Creating
Family Shabbat
Through Song

WITH MAH TOVU

RATNER MEDIA AND TECHNOLOGY CENTER
JEWISH EDUCATION CENTER OF CLEVELAND

BEHRMAN HOUSE, INC.

RMC
241
DAY
16266

Day of days : Creating family Shabbat through songs with Mah Tovu

Text: Rabbi Josh D. Zweiback and Vicki L. Weber
Songs:
  • *L'chu N'ran'nah* © 2001 by Mah Tovu (Brodsky, Chasen, and Zweiback); Original lyrics by Rabbi Ken Chasen; Music by Rabbi Ken Chasen and Rabbi Josh Zweiback.
  • *Tov L'hodot* © 2001 by Mah Tovu (Brodsky, Chasen, and Zweiback); Music and original lyrics by Rabbi Ken Chasen.
  • *Parents' Prayer* © 2001 by Mah Tovu (Brodsky, Chasen and Zweiback); Music and original lyrics by Rabbi Ken Chasen.
  • *Yism'hu* © 2003 by Mah Tovu (Brodsky, Chasen, and Zweiback); Music by Rabbi Ken Chasen and Rabbi Josh Zweiback; Lyrics from traditional liturgy.
  • *Sim Shalom* © 2001 by Mah Tovu (Brodsky, Chasen, and Zweiback); Music by Rabbi Josh Zweiback; Lyrics from traditional liturgy.
  • *Hakafah* © 2001 by Mah Tovu (Brodsky, Chasen, and Zweiback); Music by Rabbi Ken Chasen; Lyrics from traditional liturgy.
  • *The Queen* © 2003 by Mah Tovu (Brodsky, Chasen, and Zweiback); Original lyrics by Rabbi Josh Zweiback; Music by Steve Brodsky, Rabbi Ken Chasen, and Rabbi Josh Zweiback.
  • *Candle Lighting Blessing* © 1940 by Bloch Publishing, transferred to Transcontinental Music 1985; Music by A.W. Binder.
  • *Friday Night Kiddush* (P.D.) from Todah W'Simrah, 1882; Music by L. Lewandowski.
  • *Hamotzi* © 1970 by UAHC; Music by S. Adler.
Cover Art: Susan Shoshana Rama
Cover and CD Design: Susan Shoshana Rama
Project Editor: Vicki L. Weber

Copyright © 2003 by Behrman House, Inc.
ISBN 0-87441-727-9
Published by Behrman House, Inc.
www.behrmanhouse.com/family

Manufactured in the United States of America

INTRODUCTION

Day of rest. Day of freedom. First among the Holy Days. Shabbat is a day like no other. Its essence is captured by the Friday night Kiddush, which in its introduction reminds us that after six days of Creation God rested and was renewed (*shavat vayinafash*) on the seventh. The Kiddush explains that Shabbat is also *zeicher litzi'at mitzrayim*—a remembrance of our Exodus from Egypt. The central story of our Jewish heritage is that once we were slaves but now we are free. The hallmark of our freedom is Shabbat.

Shabbat is also *kadosh,* sanctified: it is separate, an island in time. The Torah tells us that God set aside this special time before setting apart either a special place or a special people. Shabbat is that important. It is our day of days.

The rituals of Shabbat can strengthen family ties and enhance our children's appreciation of their Jewish heritage. Plus, making Shabbat together is fun. Yet today's families have hectic schedules that often seem at odds with the vision of a peaceful, spiritually uplifting Shabbat. Day of Days is designed to help families bridge the gap between the real and the ideal. Whatever your knowledge or observance, its songs and suggestions can help you craft a family Shabbat experience that is both meaningful and enjoyable.

May you and your family share the beauty of this day together.

Shabbat shalom,
Josh, Ken, and Steve.

HOW TO USE THIS CD

Whether you already celebrate Shabbat weekly, or are just beginning, playing the Day of Days CD can help your entire family begin to "feel" Shabbat. The rhythms of *L'chu N'ran'nah, Yism'ḥu,* and *Hakafah* can help set the mood while you and your family prepare for Friday night, allowing everyone to become mentally ready to welcome Shabbat.

Songs around the table are part of Shabbat's joy. Lyrics to all the songs are included so you and your family can sing along. *Kavanot,* reflections, for each song explain its themes, providing an opportunity for Shabbat study. Friday night blessings, chanted by Mah Tovu, are also included so that even beginners can feel confident. A template for creating a family blessing helps you add your own personal touch.

Suggestions for activities emphasize the restorative power of spending time with the people we love. A "Countdown to Shabbat" provides a few practical ideas on how to plan (and even some simple recipes) so that busy families can feel heartened rather than harried, and closer to the peace that is the promise of Shabbat.

If it is your family's practice not to listen to recorded music on Shabbat, you can play Day of Days in preparation, as a signal that Shabbat is about to begin. After havdalah, playing *The Queen* can be the signal that a return to weekday activities is at hand.

Finally, although experiences in the home are the focus of Day of Days, Shabbat is of course also the time for Jews to gather together in the synagogue for prayer, for study, and for celebration.

KABBALAT SHABBAT
Preparing to Welcome Shabbat

According to our tradition, Shabbat is not simply a good idea, but a mitzvah. The Ten Commandments, *Aseret Hadibrot,* urge us: "Remember Shabbat and set it apart. Six days you shall toil and do all your work but the seventh day is the Shabbat of the Eternal your God" (Exodus 20:8-10).

The medieval sage Rashi focused on a curious part of the commandment: "Six days shall you toil and do all your work. . ." How, he asked, can you complete all your work in six days? In eleventh century France, Rashi understood what we still face today—that there is simply more work to get done each week than we can possibly manage. Said Rashi, "When Shabbat comes, it should seem to you as if all your work is completed. You should stop thinking about work" (Rashi on Exodus 20:9).

Our ancestors recognized that it is hard to make the transition from the six days of the work week to a day of rest. Friday evening is designed to help us perform this magic trick, to begin to act *as if* our work is done. Our transition can actually begin as early as Wednesday when, according to tradition, we may begin to wish each other *"Shabbat shalom."* In the ancient world, Thursday was a market day, when the planning for and preparation of the Sabbath meal began.

Music can help set the mood. Candles help, too, creating an atmosphere of warmth. Good food and drink make Shabbat an *oneg,* a joy. Work is set aside. The Sabbath Queen has arrived!

L'CHU N'RAN'NAH

Chorus:

לְכוּ נְרַנְּנָה
לַיְיָ
נָרִיעָה
לְצוּר יִשְׁעֵנוּ

L'chu n'ran'nah, yai lai lai lai lai
L'Adonai, yai lai lai lai lai
Nari'ah, yai lai lai lai lai
L'tzur yisheinu, yai lai lai lai lai

Let us sing out to God, the Maker of all, sure and strong.
Let all of Creation, from mountain to sea, hear our song.

Chorus

For all of the wonders in all of God's light, we rejoice.
So now let us listen with all of our hearts
To hear God's voice.

Chorus

שִׁירוּ, שִׁירוּ, שִׁיר לַיְיָ
שִׁירוּ, שִׁיר חָדָשׁ

Shiru, shiru, shir l'Adonai
Shiru, shir hadash

Come let us sing out to the Eternal, let our song ring out to our sheltering Rock (Psalm 95:1). Sing a new song to God (Psalm 96:1).

KAVANOT:
Reflections on *L'chu N'ran'nah*

Our sages taught that upon seeing a woman about to be married, one should dance before her, singing, "O beautiful and graceful bride!" We do something like this at weddings today: We crane our necks to see the bride as she approaches the *huppah*. We admire her beautiful dress, her hair, her smile. We see the love in the bridegroom's eyes and we say to ourselves, if not aloud, "What a beautiful and graceful bride!"

It may have been this understanding that shaped the Shabbat rituals of two Talmudic rabbis, Hanina and Yannai. Rabbi Hanina would dress in beautiful robes, and go outside at sunset on Friday calling, "Come let us go and welcome the Sabbath Queen!" Rabbi Yannai would call out, *"Bo'i kallah! Bo'i kallah!"* Come, O bride! Come, O bride! (Babylonian Talmud, Shabbat 119a) Thus each Shabbat is like a wedding, a joyous event celebrating the love of the Jewish people for this day.

Sixteenth century Jewish mystics created a special service, *Kabbalat Shabbat,* designed to welcome the Sabbath Bride. In creating the liturgy, these early mystics chose from among the most beautiful poems in our tradition—the Book of Psalms.

L'chu N'ran'nah, Psalm 95, is the first of these songs of welcome. As we go out to greet Shabbat, as we celebrate and remember Creation itself, how fitting it is to say: "Let us sing to Adonai! Let us make a joyful noise to the Rock of Our Salvation." This arrangement of *L'chu N'ran'nah* also includes the first line of the next psalm traditionally recited during *Kabbalat Shabbat,* Psalm 96: "O sing a new song to God!"

TOV L'HODOT

Chorus:

טוֹב לְהֹדוֹת לַיְיָ
וּלְזַמֵּר לְשִׁמְךָ עֶלְיוֹן
טוֹב לְהֹדוֹת לַיְיָ
וּלְזַמֵּר לְשִׁמְךָ עֶלְיוֹן

Tov l'hodot l'Adonai
Ul'zameir l'shimcha Elyon
Tov l'hodot l'Adonai
Ul'zameir l'shimcha Elyon

On this, the Day of Days, my lips shall sing Your praise,
For I know that You'll always be here surrounding me.

Chorus

My spirit takes release, I close my eyes in peace,
And from my soul, heard far above,
Springs a song of love.

Chorus

I wish to understand the wonders of Your hand.
For all the blessings that are mine rise from Your design.

Chorus

It is good to praise the Eternal, to sing hymns to Your name, O Most High (Psalm 92:2).

KAVANOT:
Reflections on *Tov L'hodot*

Jewish tradition has always had ways to mark the significance of time. For example, the Talmud tells us that the Levites, the Temple priests, would sing a different psalm for each day of the week and for each of the Holy Days during the year. Rabbi Akiva, the great sage of the second century, explained that each psalm corresponds to an aspect of God's Creation for that particular day of the week. Thus every day we are reminded of God's Creation, of our place in the universe.

Psalm 92 is the psalm traditionally assigned to Shabbat. The connection becomes obvious with its very first line:

מִזְמוֹר שִׁיר לְיוֹם הַשַּׁבָּת.

Mizmor shir l'yom hashabat.
A poetic song for the Sabbath day.

The second verse, which this song is based upon, is in some ways the ultimate expression of gratitude—a prayer of thanksgiving for the privilege of giving thanks:

טוֹב לְהֹדוֹת לַייָ וּלְזַמֵּר לְשִׁמְךָ עֶלְיוֹן!

Tov l'hodot l'Adonai, ul'zameir l'shimcha Elyon!
How good to thank Adonai, to sing to Your Exalted Name!

Shabbat is a time to reflect upon the goodness in our lives, to appreciate the wonders of Creation and the gifts of family and friends, and then to sing out "Thank You!" with all of our heart.

PARENTS' PRAYER

Here with you beside me, I feel so greatly blessed,
This moment means much more than I can say.
A time to be together, a time for us to rest,
Shabbat is here, the time has come to celebrate the day.
So I hold you close, my hands upon your head,
And from me to you, my child, these words are said:

Chorus:

יְשִׂמְךָ אֱלֹהִים כְּאֶפְרַיִם וְכִמְנַשֶּׁה.

Y'simcha Elohim k'Efrayim v'chiM'nasheh
May God give you life and strength
Like Joseph's sons.

יְשִׂמֵךְ אֱלֹהִים כְּשָׂרָה, רִבְקָה, רָחֵל, וְלֵאָה.

Y'simeich Elohim k'Sarah, Rivkah, Raḥeil, v'Lei'ah
May God make you like our mothers,
like our blessed ones.

As I watch you growing, I smile through my tears;
Sometimes I wish you'd stay forever small.
But then I see you blossom,
And I befriend the passing years.
I love you now, I'll love you then—I love to see it all.
So I lift my voice to offer you this prayer,
For every step along the road, I will be there.

Chorus

May God make you like our parents,
like our blessed ones.

KAVANOT:
Reflections on *Parents' Prayer*

The book of Genesis is filled with stories about family—stories ultimately about *our* family, the people Israel. As with most family stories, some are sad, some are filled with hope, and some describe great despair. Many are profoundly moving.

Every Friday evening we remember in particular the story of Jacob, his son Joseph, and his grandsons, Ephraim and Menasseh. We recall that Joseph was sold into slavery by his jealous brothers. They let their father Jacob believe that he had been killed by a wild animal. Years later, after much turmoil and pain, the family was reunited and the brothers reconciled.

Just before he died, Jacob gave his grandsons, Ephraim and Menasseh, a special blessing. Holding them close, he told them that one day all the Jewish people would bless their own sons saying, "May God make you like Ephraim and Menasseh" (Genesis 48:20). He seemed to say, "Despite the rivalry, deception and disappointment our family has faced, the Jewish people will someday come together, united through this special prayer. They will express their deepest wishes: that their children will be a blessing, and that their families will be whole."

The sages later added a blessing for Jewish daughters, asking God to make them like the founding mothers of our people: Sarah, Rebecca, Rachel, and Leah.

At its core, Shabbat is a time for family. This special prayer is inspired by the hope that our own personal family stories will be filled with love, light, joy, goodness, and harmony.

CREATE YOUR OWN FAMILY BLESSING

You can finish the following sentences to create your own family Shabbat blessing. The idea banks provide suggestions, but feel free to come up with your own.

Adonai our God, God of all generations, bless our family. Grant us _____ (idea bank: strength, harmony, closeness, joy, friendship), **and make us like our ancestors, Ephraim and Menasseh, Sarah, Rebecca, Rachel and Leah.**

As we turn from the work and school week just ended, and welcome Shabbat, help us take the time to _____ (idea bank: be together, enjoy Your world, restore ourselves, find inspiration). **We thank You for Your precious gift—the gift of Shabbat. Amen.**

SHIFTING GEARS

We can play the songs on this CD to help set the mood for Shabbat. We can light the candles and say the blessings over wine and bread. But we can also shift gears by spending time on Friday night reviewing the week that just ended.

The Week That Was. During dinner, have each person around the table describe something significant that happened during the past week. You can choose a theme: "This week's best moment"; "My accomplishment"; or "Something new I learned this week." Or, you can focus on family harmony by having each person name something special another family member said or did during the week. With older children, each person can choose a news event of the past week, and describe his or her view of how it could serve as a call to action to help repair the world.

YOM SHABBAT
Restoring Ourselves through Shabbat

The concept of a day of rest was alien to most ancient peoples. The Greeks and Romans, for example, ridiculed this peculiar Jewish institution, accusing our ancestors of laziness, of indolence, for resting one day out of every seven. But while Shabbat is called *yom m'nuha*, a day of rest, it would be a mistake to think of it as a "lazy day." *M'nuha* means much more than refraining from work or simply taking it easy. *M'nuha* is restorative. It recharges us spiritually as well as physically.

So how do we experience this rejuvenating rest? It should come as no surprise that, for our sages, the ideal way to restore the soul and refresh the spirit was through Torah study. As Hillel taught, "The more Torah, the more life!" (Pirkei Avot 2:7). Shabbat is an invitation to make time for learning, whether it is reading a Jewish book or magazine, attending synagogue services, or studying the weekly Torah portion with your family.

The rabbis of the Talmud understood that by dedicating a day to *m'nuha*, we also celebrate our freedom. They called it *zeicher litzi'at mitzrayim,* a remembrance of the Exodus from Egypt. Shabbat should free us to spend more time with our families, to enjoy just being together, savoring the small moments that usually pass unnoticed.

Shabbat is, as one sage calls it, *matanah tovah,* a precious gift. Indeed it is, restoring the body as well as the soul, freeing us to reflect on what matters most.

YISM'ḤU

Chorus:
Yism'ḥu v'malchut'cha,
Shomrei shabat,
Shomrei shabat
V'korei oneg.

יִשְׂמְחוּ בְמַלְכוּתְךָ,
שׁוֹמְרֵי שַׁבָּת,
שׁוֹמְרֵי שַׁבָּת
וְקוֹרְאֵי עֹנֶג.

עַם מְקַדְּשֵׁי, מְקַדְּשֵׁי שְׁבִיעִי,
כֻּלָּם יִשְׂבְּעוּ וְיִתְעַנְּגוּ מִטּוּבֶךָ.

Am m'kadshei, m'kadshei, sh'vi'i,
Kulam yisb'u v'yitangu mituvecha.

Chorus

וְהַשְּׁבִיעִי רָצִיתָ בּוֹ וְקִדַּשְׁתּוֹ,
חֶמְדַּת יָמִים אוֹתוֹ קָרָאתָ,

V'hashvi'i ratzita bo v'kidashto,
Ḥemdat yamim oto karata,

זֵכֶר לְמַעֲשֵׂה בְרֵאשִׁית.

Zeicher l'ma'asei v'reishit.

Chorus

Those who observe Shabbat and call it a delight will rejoice in Your Sovereignty. The people that sets apart the seventh day will be completely satisfied by Your goodness. For You have set apart the seventh day, calling it the most desired of days, a reminder of the works of Creation.

KAVANOT:
Reflections on Yism'ḥu

Yism'ḥu means "rejoice." The prayer, which is inserted on Shabbat during the Amidah (the central section of prayers in every worship service), calls our attention to the joy we can derive from treating Shabbat as a day set apart from the others in our week.

The Yism'ḥu prayer tells us that God called Shabbat ḥemdat yamim, literally "the coveted of all days." Rabbi Abraham Joshua Heschel, the noted twentieth century Jewish thinker, pointed out the apparent contradiction between the idea of a coveted day and the Tenth Commandment, lo taḥmod, "you shall not covet" (Exodus 20:14). Heschel's conclusion was that the only thing we are permitted (even commanded) to covet is Shabbat. The joy of Shabbat, the delight we take in this special time of reflection, renewal, and celebration, is to be coveted, craved, valued above all else.

In a culture in which we are bombarded unceasingly by messages designed to ignite material desires, Shabbat provides the opportunity to realign ourselves. By setting Shabbat apart, we embrace sacred time, time to pause and turn our attention to eternal values—friendship, family, learning, peace, and love.

Rejoice in Shabbat's goodness. Call it a delight. Covet it.

SIM SHALOM

Chorus:
Sim shalom, שִׂים שָׁלוֹם,
Tovah uv'rachah, טוֹבָה וּבְרָכָה,
Hein vahesed v'rahamim, חֵן וָחֶסֶד וְרַחֲמִים,
Aleinu v'al kol yisra'el עָלֵינוּ וְעַל־כָּל־יִשְׂרָאֵל
Amecha. עַמֶּךָ.

V'tov b'einecha וְטוֹב בְּעֵינֶיךָ
L'vareich et am'cha yisra'el לְבָרֵךְ אֶת־עַמְּךָ יִשְׂרָאֵל
B'chol eit uv'chol sha'ah בְּכָל־עֵת וּבְכָל־שָׁעָה
Bish'lomecha. בִּשְׁלוֹמֶךָ.

Chorus

Baruch Atah, Adonai, בָּרוּךְ אַתָּה, יְיָ,
Ham'vareich et amo הַמְבָרֵךְ אֶת־עַמּוֹ
Yisra'el bashalom, bashalom. יִשְׂרָאֵל בַּשָּׁלוֹם, בַּשָּׁלוֹם.

Chorus

Grant peace, goodness and blessing, grace and love, and mercy, to us and to all Your people Israel. May it be good in Your eyes to bless Your people Israel at all times with Your peace. Blessed are You, Eternal our God, who blesses Your people Israel with peace.

KAVANOT:
Reflections on *Sim Shalom*

Every prayer service within our tradition includes prayers for peace. The blessings after each meal conclude with the hope that the One who makes peace in the heavens will also make peace on earth. These prayers give voice to our yearning for that which at times seems the most unattainable thing on earth.

Sim Shalom is one of these prayers. It is found in the concluding section of the morning and afternoon Amidah. Its words can help guide us to a full understanding of the meaning of shalom, peace. For at its most basic, *shalom* means "completeness," and it includes "goodness, blessing, grace, compassion and mercy." *Sim Shalom* beseeches God, the Maker of Peace, to grant the Jewish people the greatest blessing imaginable: not riches, not strength, not fame, but shalom—wholeness, completeness, peace.

Shabbat provides the opportunity to taste peace. By engaging ourselves and our families in a time of self-reflection, rejuvenation, study, and the enjoyment of the world, we can experience weekly the thing we ask for the most often.

Through our prayers we constantly remind ourselves of the importance of peace and our unceasing desire for it. We experience it for ourselves on Shabbat. And then, most importantly, inspired by our words, refreshed by our rest, we can go forth to try with all our might to make peace a reality.

HAKAFAH

Yai, lai, lai . . .

בֵּית יַעֲקֹב לְכוּ וְנֵלְכָה
לְכוּ וְנֵלְכָה בְּאוֹר יְיָ.
יִשְׂרָאֵל וְאוֹרַיְתָא וְקֻדְשָׁא
בְּרִיךְ הוּא חַד הוּא.

Beit Ya'akov l'chu v'neil'chah
L'chu v'neil'chah b'or Adonai.
Yisrael v'orayta v'kudsha
B'rich hu ḥad hu.

Yai, lai, lai . . .

כִּי מִצִּיּוֹן תֵּצֵא תוֹרָה, וּדְבַר יְיָ מִירוּשָׁלָיִם.
בָּרוּךְ שֶׁנָּתַן תּוֹרָה, תּוֹרָה לְעַמּוֹ יִשְׂרָאֵל בִּקְדֻשָּׁתוֹ.

Ki mitziyon teitzei torah ud'var Adonai miyrushalayim.
Baruch shenatan torah, torah l'amo yisrael bik'dushato.

Yai, lai, lai . . .

תּוֹרָה אוֹרָה הַלְלוּיָהּ.

Torah orah hal'luyah.

O house of Jacob, come let us walk by the light of the Eternal. Israel, Torah and God are one! For Torah will go forth from Zion, and the word of the Eternal from Jerusalem. Blessed is the One who has given Torah to the people of Israel in holiness. Torah is light. Halleluyah!

KAVANOT:
Reflections on *Hakafah*

Hakafah celebrates the central importance of Torah for Jews, highlighting the joy, and ultimately the peace, that studying Torah brings us. Literally translated as "to walk around" or "to circle," *Hakafah* is traditionally sung as we remove the Torah from the Ark and parade among the congregation during Shabbat morning services.

As the Torah procession begins, we sing, "O House of Jacob, come let us go out in the Light of the Eternal" (Isaiah 2:5). Elsewhere in the Bible we learn, "Torah is light" (Proverbs 6:23). The sages understood the verse to mean: "O Jewish people, it is time to take the Torah out to read and study!"

The Book of Isaiah, the source of several of the verses, tells us that studying and living Torah will bring peace to the world. Isaiah prophesies that the time will come when all nations shall gather in Jerusalem at Mt. Zion to study Torah. And what will be the result of their learning? According to Isaiah, "Then they shall beat their swords into plowshares and their spears into pruning hooks. Nation shall not lift up sword against nation, and they shall never again know war" (Isaiah 2:4).

For Isaiah then, the end result of Torah study is shalom. When we remember his words we remind ourselves of the true purpose of our learning: to bring completeness to ourselves, our families, our communities, and all the world. Realizing this, we thank God, the Source of this great truth, singing, "Blessed is the One who gave Torah to the People Israel."

FAMILY TIME ON SHABBAT

A family activity unique to Shabbat can take on the quality of ritual, enhancing the feeling of a time set apart. Some of these ideas can emerge spontaneously; others may require advance planning. And remember, these are just to get you thinking. The best family rituals are those we create for ourselves.

Boker Tov. Greet Shabbat morning with a family snuggle. Pick a bedroom, add some orange juice, a little music, reading time, or a quiet game. You may wish to add a family blessing to start the day.

Share Shabbat. With your children, create coupons that family members can redeem on Shabbat. Each should be good for a special Shabbat-friendly activity that the recipient particularly enjoys (an uninterrupted bubble bath; a backrub; reading a favorite story or playing a game of checkers with a parent).

Time in a Bottle. On slips of paper, have each person write down a favorite Shabbat family activity, one per slip. Keep the papers in a jar and on Shabbat, pick one out. Your afternoon family activity, whether it is taking a hike or flying a kite, is all arranged. Set this week's slip aside so that everyone's eventually is chosen.

Who am I? Add a little Torah to the mix with an identity guessing game. One person gives a short description of a biblical figure, while the others try to guess who it is. The first person with the correct answer gives the next set of clues. Example: I tried to run away from God but was swallowed by a fish. Who am I? (Answer: Jonah). Beware: Youngsters may be driven to a little extra research to try to stump the grownups.

Y'TZI'AT SHABBAT
Bidding Farewell to Shabbat

Ancient peoples measured time according to the rhythms of the sun and moon, the changes in the seasons. Yet what is there in the physical realm that describes a week? Setting aside every seventh day as the Sabbath was an invention independent of changes in the sun's position or the moon's appearance. It created an awareness beyond that of physical surroundings; an awareness of time itself.

Heschel famously called Shabbat "a palace in time." By marking the separation between Shabbat and the rest of the week, we remind ourselves that it is the time that is holy. Our ritual goodbye helps preserve the distinction that is the essential nature of Shabbat.

SELECTED HAVDALAH BLESSINGS

To perform havdalah, you will need a Kiddush cup, wine or grape juice, at least two kinds of spices placed in a container, a braided havdalah candle, and matches.

Raise the lit candle and lift the filled cup, saying:

בָּרוּךְ אַתָּה, יְיָ אֱלֹהֵינוּ, מֶלֶךְ הָעוֹלָם,
בּוֹרֵא פְּרִי הַגָּפֶן.

Baruch Atah, Adonai Eloheinu, Melech ha'olam,
borei p'ri hagafen.
Blessed are you, Adonai our God, Ruler of the world, who creates the fruit of the vine.

Without drinking, set the cup down.

Next, lift the spice box, saying:

בָּרוּךְ אַתָּה, יְיָ אֱלֹהֵינוּ, מֶלֶךְ הָעוֹלָם, בּוֹרֵא מִינֵי בְשָׂמִים.

Baruch Atah, Adonai Eloheinu, Melech ha'olam,
borei minei v'samim.
Blessed are You, Adonai our God, Ruler of the world, who creates the varieties of spices.

Pass the spice box for each person to inhale the scent. Then say:

בָּרוּךְ אַתָּה, יְיָ אֱלֹהֵינוּ, מֶלֶךְ הָעוֹלָם, בּוֹרֵא מְאוֹרֵי הָאֵשׁ.

Baruch Atah, Adonai Eloheinu, Melech ha'olam,
borei m'orei ha'eish.
Blessed are You, Adonai our God, Ruler of the world, who creates the fiery lights.

Hold your hands in front of the candlelight so you can see the flame in the reflection of your fingernails as well as the shadows cast by your fingers on your palms, illustrating the distinction between light and dark.
Then say:

בָּרוּךְ אַתָּה, יְיָ, הַמַּבְדִּיל בֵּין קֹדֶשׁ לְחוֹל.

Baruch Atah, Adonai, hamavdil bein kodesh l'hol.
Blessed are you, Adonai, who separates the sacred from the ordinary.

Take a sip of the wine, then extinguish the flame in the cup with the remaining wine. S*havua tov—A good week!*

THE QUEEN

Yai, dai, dai . . .
Evening falls
The sun has set
And the Queen has gone away
The time has come
Once again
To say thank You, we thank You
For this day

Yai, dai, dai . . .
Well of joy
The Day of Days
May her blessings never cease
Let her return
Every week
To embrace us, embrace us
With her peace

Look inside
The secret's there
By her light we'll someday see
How You and I
Make the day
Of redemption, redemption
Come to be

בָּרוּךְ אַתָּה יְיָ, אֱלֹהֵינוּ מֶלֶךְ הָעוֹלָם,
הַמַּבְדִּיל בֵּין קֹדֶשׁ לְחוֹל.

Baruch Atah Adonai, Eloheinu Melech ha'olam,
hamavdil bein kodesh l'ḥol.
Yai, dai, dai . . .

Blessed are You, Adonai our God, Ruler of the world, who separates the sacred from the ordinary.

KAVANOT:
Reflections on *The Queen*

Although he probably wasn't thinking about havdalah, Shakespeare described it perfectly when he wrote: "Parting is such sweet sorrow."

Saying goodbye to Shabbat is indeed bittersweet for it marks the return to ordinary time—to the work-a-day world filled with tasks, deadlines, and stress. But Shabbat happens every week, so our regret is tempered by the realization that in just six days, the Sabbath Queen will return.

Our rabbis created havdalah (literally "distinction" or "separation") over 2,000 years ago in order to make this transition easier. We give thanks to God for making Shabbat different from the other days of the week by employing certain symbols that both remind us of the goodness we have enjoyed and point us toward a more hopeful future. Wine and fragrant spices represent the sweetness and joy of Shabbat. The braided candle symbolizes the bright, warm light that Shabbat brings to our lives. It also reminds us of how Shabbat brings us together, the many wicks combining into one flame.

At the end of the havdalah ceremony, we evoke the memory of Elijah the Prophet who, according to tradition, is the herald of the messianic age, a time when universal peace will reign. This is meant to inspire us to go out into the world of the everyday and perform *tikkun olam*, actions to repair the world. For it is in this way, our tradition says, that we and God together will bring about the time called *yom shekulo Shabbat*, "the Ultimate Sabbath," when everyday will be Shabbat.

SHABBAT SHALOM
Preparing for the Next Shabbat

Glowing candles, cheerful faces, heartfelt blessings, a good dinner, the joy of song: This is the vision we as parents conjure for ourselves when we vow to make family Shabbat a more central event in our lives. At the end of a busy week, however, what we often confront are tired spouses, cranky children, and the complicated logistics of bringing everyone together around an evening meal. Rather than feeling imbued with the peace of Shabbat, we can easily feel burdened. How then, do we help our families "feel" Shabbat?

Traditionally, we Jews have marked our days in relation to Shabbat. Thus, one would either be saying goodbye to the Shabbat just ended by using the greeting s*havua tov,* a good week, or, beginning on Wednesday, looking forward to the coming Shabbat and wishing all *Shabbat shalom.* Anticipation, and the planning it engenders, would help everyone be prepared for Shabbat's arrival.

COUNTDOWN TO SHABBAT

Prior to every space launch, a clock is kept at mission control. Everyone knows just when the journey is supposed to begin, and each has a part to play in getting ready. Our preparations for Shabbat, whether elaborate or simple, can help us get both our homes and our psyches ready for our own weekly journey.

You can create your own family countdown to Shabbat by involving everyone in the planning and preparation, from baking (or buying) ḥallah, to setting the table. The routine of getting ready is transformed into a family ritual that prepares all for the arrival of Shabbat.

Create a Shabbat Menu. Whether it is homemade chicken soup or take-out Chinese, a favorite food can add to the enjoyment of Shabbat. Gather ideas to plan your own special meal. The matzah balls on page 26 take only ten minutes to mix, and the broth can be your own or the market's. When making the shopping list, don't forget staples such as candles, wine, and grape juice. Have each family member sign up for a task: who will help shop; who will help cook (or pick up the pizza).

Hello Hallah. Making hallah is a great way to involve children in Shabbat preparations. The recipe on page 25 takes only half an hour to mix on Thursday evening and fifteen minutes to braid on Friday, plus an hour to rise and bake. Not a baker but want warm bread? Excellent frozen, unbaked hallah is available in many supermarkets. Of course, a weekly trip to your favorite bakery for hallah is wonderful ritual in its own right.

Set a Special Table. Involve everyone in setting the table. Choose items to set your Shabbat meal apart, whether it is Bubbie's heirloom china or pretty paper plates. Playing Day of Days while you work adds to the Shabbat mood. Last one home brings the flowers!

Personalize Your Rituals. A homemade tzedakah box, a candlestick or Kiddush cup for each family member, kippot collected from the b'nai mitzvah ceremonies of family and friends: Collect ritual objects with beauty and meaning for your family and bring them out for Shabbat.

Guess Who's Coming to Dinner. As children grow older, the Friday night social attractions increase. One way to keep them happy at home is to make Friday night "Bring a Friend for Shabbat Dinner" night. When they know that even their impromptu guests are welcome, children (and especially teens) can begin to make Shabbat celebration their own.

ḤALLAH

This is a two-part recipe; the dough must be refrigerated overnight. Makes two loaves.

1 package dry yeast	3 eggs, lightly beaten
1/4 cup plus 2 tbsp sugar	1/3 cup oil
1 cup lukewarm water	1/2 cup warm water
5 cups flour	1 1/4 to 1 1/2 cups flour
1 tbsp plus 1 tsp salt	1 egg, lightly beaten

ON THURSDAY: *(30 min. active time; 1 hr. rising time)*
- Add yeast and sugar to 1 cup of lukewarm water and stir until dissolved.
- Put 5 cups of flour into a large bowl. Make a well in the flour and add salt, 3 eggs, oil, and yeast mixture. Mix thoroughly.
- Add 1/2 cup warm water. Stir in additional 1 1/4 to 1 1/2 cups of flour to make a stiff yet easy-to-handle dough.
- Turn the dough out onto a floured surface and knead for several minutes until dough is smooth, sprinkling in more flour if dough is sticky.
- Grease a large glass bowl. Place the dough in it, turning once so both sides are greased. Cover with a towel and let the dough rise in a warm place for 1 hour.
- Punch down the dough, cover it with plastic wrap and a towel. Refrigerate overnight.

ON FRIDAY: *(15 min. active time; 60-70 min. rising and baking time)*
- Remove dough from refrigerator, punch down, and divide into six pieces. Roll each piece into a long strip, then braid three strips together to make a loaf, pinching the strips together at each end. Braid the remaining three strips and pinch the ends to make a second loaf.
- Cover and let rise for 30-40 minutes in a warm place. Brush each loaf lightly with a beaten egg. Bake at 350 degrees for 30-35 minutes until golden brown. To test

for doneness, a thump on the bottom should give a hollow sound.

Hallah is Taken. The Hebrew word *hallah* actually refers not to the loaf itself, but to the ancient command to set aside a portion of bread for the Temple priests. After the Temple's destruction, it became customary to take a small part of the dough and throw it into the fire to represent this portion. If you wish to fulfill this mitzvah in your own baking for Shabbat, pinch off an olive-sized piece of dough before baking, and put it under the broiler until it blackens. The blessing is: "Blessed are You, Adonai our God, Ruler of the world, who has commanded us to separate the hallah from the dough."

MATZAH BALLS
Makes approximately 16 matzah balls
(10 min. active time; 1 hr resting time; 20-25 min. cooking time)

2 eggs
1/4 cup water
3 tablespoons vegetable oil
1 teaspoon salt
dash of pepper
1/2 cup matzah meal

Beat eggs slightly with a fork. Add the water, vegetable oil, salt, and pepper. Mix well. Add the matzah meal and stir thoroughly. Refrigerate for 1 hour.

Wet your hands and form the mixture into small balls. Drop balls into a large pot of boiling water. Cover and simmer 20-25 minutes. Remove from water and serve immediately in bowls of hot chicken or vegetable broth.

FRIDAY NIGHT BLESSINGS

You can sing along with Mah Tovu on the CD as they chant the candle blessing, Kiddush, and the blessing over the bread. For your children, use the blessing below or create one of your own (see page 10).

LIGHTING THE CANDLES. Traditionally, just before sunset, we light at least two candles to welcome Shabbat. After lighting the candles, move your hands around the flames three times, then cover your eyes and recite the blessing.

בָּרוּךְ אַתָּה, יְיָ אֱלֹהֵינוּ,
מֶלֶךְ הָעוֹלָם,
אֲשֶׁר קִדְּשָׁנוּ
בְּמִצְוֹתָיו וְצִוָּנוּ
לְהַדְלִיק נֵר שֶׁל שַׁבָּת.

Baruch Atah, Adonai Eloheinu,
Melech ha'olam,
asher kid'shanu
b'mitzvotav v'tzivanu
l'hadlik neir shel shabat.

Blessed are You, Adonai our God, Ruler of the world, who makes us holy with Your mitzvot, and commands us to light the Shabbat candles.

BLESSING THE CHILDREN. Place your hands on your child's head and say:
For daughters:

יְשִׂמֵךְ אֱלֹהִים כְּשָׂרָה, רִבְקָה, רָחֵל, וְלֵאָה.

Y'simeich Elohim k'Sarah, Rivkah, Raḥeil, v'Lei'ah.
May God make you like Sarah, Rebecca, Rachel, and Leah.

For sons:

יְשִׂמְךָ אֱלֹהִים כְּאֶפְרַיִם וְכִמְנַשֶּׁה.

Y'simcha Elohim k'Efrayim v'chiM'nasheh.
May God make you like Ephraim and Menasseh.

For all children:

יְבָרֶכְךָ יְיָ וְיִשְׁמְרֶךָ.
יָאֵר יְיָ פָּנָיו אֵלֶיךָ וִיחֻנֶּךָּ.
יִשָּׂא יְיָ פָּנָיו אֵלֶיךָ וְיָשֵׂם לְךָ שָׁלוֹם.

Y'varech'cha Adonai v'yishm'recha.
Ya'eir Adonai panav eilecha vi'huneka.
Yisa Adonai panav eilecha v'yaseim l'cha shalom.

May God bless you and keep you. May God's light shine upon you. May God's face be lifted upon you and give you peace.

FRIDAY NIGHT KIDDUSH. Hold the filled wine cup in your right hand as you recite the blessings:

בָּרוּךְ אַתָּה, יְיָ אֱלֹהֵינוּ,
מֶלֶךְ הָעוֹלָם,
בּוֹרֵא פְּרִי הַגָּפֶן.

Baruch Atah, Adonai Eloheinu,
Melech ha'olam borei p'ri hagafen.

Blessed are You, Adonai our God, Ruler of the World, who creates the fruit of the vine.

בָּרוּךְ אַתָּה, יְיָ אֱלֹהֵינוּ, מֶלֶךְ הָעוֹלָם, אֲשֶׁר קִדְּשָׁנוּ בְּמִצְוֹתָיו וְרָצָה בָנוּ, וְשַׁבַּת קָדְשׁוֹ בְּאַהֲבָה וּבְרָצוֹן הִנְחִילָנוּ, זִכָּרוֹן לְמַעֲשֵׂה בְרֵאשִׁית. כִּי הוּא יוֹם תְּחִלָּה לְמִקְרָאֵי קֹדֶשׁ, זֵכֶר לִיצִיאַת מִצְרָיִם. כִּי־בָנוּ בָחַרְתָּ

וְאוֹתָנוּ קִדַּשְׁתָּ מִכָּל־הָעַמִּים, וְשַׁבַּת קָדְשְׁךָ בְּאַהֲבָה וּבְרָצוֹן הִנְחַלְתָּנוּ. בָּרוּךְ אַתָּה, יְיָ, מְקַדֵּשׁ הַשַּׁבָּת.

Baruch Atah, Adonai Eloheinu, Melech ha'olam, asher kid'shanu b'mitzvotav v'ratzah vanu, v'shabat kodsho b'ahavah uv'ratzon hinhilanu, zikaron l'ma'asei v'reishit. Ki hu yom t'hilah l'mikra'ei kodesh, zeicher litzi'at mitzrayim. Ki vanu vaharta v'otanu kidashta mikol ha'amim, v'shabat kodsh'cha b'ahavah uv'ratzon hinhaltanu. Baruch Atah, Adonai, m'kadeish hashabat.

Blessed are You, Adonai our God, Ruler of the world, who makes us holy with Your mitzvot and shows us love by giving us Your sacred Shabbat, which recalls the work of Creation. This day is the first among holy days, recalling our going forth from Egypt. You have chosen us and made us holy, and You have shown us Your love by giving us Your holy Shabbat as our heritage. Blessed are you, Adonai, who sanctifies Shabbat.

Take a sip of the wine (or juice).

HAMOTZI: BLESSING OVER BREAD. The hallah is covered with a cloth until just before the blessing is recited. Afterward, everyone takes a small piece to eat.

בָּרוּךְ אַתָּה, יְיָ אֱלֹהֵינוּ,
מֶלֶךְ הָעוֹלָם,
הַמּוֹצִיא לֶחֶם מִן הָאָרֶץ.

Baruch Atah, Adonai Eloheinu,
Melech ha'olam, hamotzi lehem min ha'aretz.

Blessed are You, Adonai our God, Ruler of the world, who brings forth bread from the earth.

MUSICAL CREDITS
All songs produced and arranged by Gordon Lustig

L'chu N'ran'nah, Tov L'hodot, Parents' Prayer, Sim Shalom, Hakafah © 2001 Mah Tovu (Brodsky/Chasen/Zweiback); *Yism'hu, The Queen* © 2003 Mah Tovu (Brodksy/Chasen/Zweiback); *Candle Lighting Blessing* ©1940 Bloch Publishing, transferred to Transcontinental Music 1985; *Friday Night Kiddush* P.D., from Todah W'Simrah, 1882; *Hamotzi* © 1970 UAHC.

L'chu N'ran'nah: **Vocals:** Ken, Josh, and Steve; **Acoustic Guitar:** Gordon Lustig; **Bass:** Kevin Axt; **Percussion:** Debra Dobkin; **Bandolim:** Michael Limpert; **Synth Programming:** Gordon Lustig.

Tov L'hodot: **Vocals:** Ken, Josh, and Steve; **Acoustic Guitar:** Ken Chasen; **Synth Programming:** Gordon Lustig; **Trumpets:** Dan Fornero; **Trombones:** Art Velasco; **French Horns:** Rachel Berry.

Parents' Prayer: **Vocals:** Ken, Josh, and Steve; **Acoustic Guitar:** Ken Chasen; **Violin:** Cameron Patrick; **Viola:** Peggy Baldwin; **Oboe:** Chris Bleth.

Yism'hu: **Vocals:** Ken, Josh, Steve; **Drums:** Chris Sandoval; **Fiddle:** Mike Tatar; **Banjo:** Alan Arnopole; **Bass:** J.V. T'nayti; **Guitar:** Gordon Lustig.

Sim Shalom: **Vocals:** Josh, Ken, and Steve; **Acoustic Guitars:** Gordon Lustig, Tom Bethke; **Bass:** Ron Sures; **Drums:** Jeff Stern; **Piano:** Wally Minko; **Synth Programming:** Gordon Lustig.

Hakafah: **Vocals:** Josh, Ken, Steve, and the Ah-Men Chorus; **Vocal Improvization:** Ken Chasen, Debra Dobkin; **Guitar:** Gordon Lustig; **Bass:** Kevin Axt; **Drums:** Bill Severance; **Percussion:** Debra Dobkin; **Duduk and Bansuri:** Chris Bleth; **Synth Programming:** Gordon Lustig.

The Queen: **Vocals:** Steve, Josh, and Ken; **Guest Vocalist:** Shirona; **Percussion:** M.B. Gordy; **Bass:** J.V. T'nayti; **Guitar:** Gordon Lustig.

Candle Lighting Blessing: **Vocals:** Steve Brodsky. *Friday Night Kiddush:* **Vocals:** Ken Chasen. *Hamotzi:* **Vocals:** Josh Zweiback.

Mah Tovu Thanks: Vicki Weber for her vision and creativity; David Behrman for making this project possible; Gordon Lustig for his immense talent and skill; Jacqueline Hantgan, Jill Katchen, and Allison Lee for their love and support; and Ariela, Benjamin B., Benjamin C., Isa, and Micah for joy, laughter, inspiration, and for making Shabbat family time.

For information on Mah Tovu, go to www.mahtovu.com